Mandela

A LIFE

SUNBIRD
PUBLISHERS

2 4 6 8 10 9 7 5 3 1
First published 2007
Sunbird Publishers (Pty) Ltd
PO Box 6836, Roggebaai, 8012
Cape Town, South Africa

www.sunbirdpublishers.co.za

Registration number: 4850177827
Copyright © 2007 published edition: Sunbird Publishers
Copyright © 2007 text: Adrian Hadland (body text)
and Sean Fraser (captions)
Copyright © 2007 photographs: as credited on page 96

Publisher Natanya Mulholland
Managing Editor Sean Fraser
Designer Mandy McKay
Picture Researcher Farieda Classen
Production Manager Andrew de Kock

Reproduction by Resolution (Pty) Ltd, Cape Town
Printed and bound by Tien Wah Press (Pte) Ltd,
Malaysia

ISBN 1 91993 860 5
13-digit ISBN 9 781 91993 860 8

preface

FEW POLITICIANS in the history of the world have attracted such widespread veneration as is bestowed on the figure of Nelson Rolihlahla Mandela. This is all the more remarkable in an age when technology and the ever-present media ensure hardly a breath is taken by an international figure that is not instantly captured and commented on. But, in spite of the attention of the world since he walked free from prison on 11 February 1990 and the rigours of accepting the presidency of what was one of the globe's most divided nations, Mandela's reputation remains as impressive as it is unsullied.

Mandela has become synonymous with the triumph of the human spirit. His name will forever speak of his capacity for suffering, of victory over adversity, of patience, forgiveness and a steadfast, iron-clad conviction that principles will always endure. As he told the Old Synagogue Court in 1962 while facing charges of leaving the country illegally, 'To men, freedom in their own land is the pinnacle of their ambitions, from which nothing can turn men of conviction aside.' The qualities of character, courage, humility and compassion that are personified in Mandela have granted him an authentic, contemporary moral authority. He is, in the words of his official biographer Anthony Sampson, 'a universal hero'.

ADRIAN HADLAND

▶ NELSON MANDELA: 'There is no easy to walk to freedom anywhere, and many of us will have to pass through the valley of the shadow of death again and again before we reach the mountain tops of our desires.'

Nelson Mandela
a portrait in words and pictures

▲ The dapper young Nelson Rolihlahla Mandela, aged 19 or 20 years old.

▼ Lovedale College, or Fort Hare, was where the young Mandela spent his early days as a student.

LIKE SO MANY HEROES, Mandela's origins are to be found in the humblest of circumstances. On the day of his birth, 18 July 1918, his home in the village of Mvezo in what is now South Africa's Eastern Cape province consisted of three mud huts: one for sleeping, one for cooking and one for storing food. Each of the huts had been crafted by the hands of his mother, Nosekeni Fanny, from soil moulded into bricks. In the living hut, which Mandela shared with his two sisters, chairs and cupboards were made from soil. There were no beds or tables, and the family slept on mats. The roof was made of bales of dried grass tied together with rope.

Mandela's father, Hendry, had four wives of whom Nosekeni was the third. He was a strict, stubborn, illiterate man who was both tall and proud. Royal blood from the Thembu people ran through his veins. The year after Mandela was born, Hendry was stripped of his chieftainship after a quarrel with the local white magistrate over an ox. Hendry refused to budge from his stance and consequently lost most of his cattle, land and income. No longer able to provide for his four wives and 13 children, he was forced to break up the family. He sent Nosekeni to live in the village of Qunu. It was here that Mandela, whose given name at birth was Rolihlahla (which means 'pulling the branch of a tree' or troublemaker) spent most of his childhood.

Mandela recalls his years at Qunu with nostalgia. His memories of swimming in rock pools, of drinking warm milk straight from the udder, of the traditional stick fights with his peers and of the overwhelming beauty of the gently undulating, verdant countryside of the Transkei were to keep his spirits high during some of his bleakest moments. For Mandela, home will always be Qunu. It was at school in Qunu that Mandela was given the name of Nelson. It was a common practice for children educated in mission schools at that time to be given an English name, very often that of a British imperial hero.

On the premature death of his father, the nine-year-old Mandela was adopted by his uncle, Jongintaba Dalindyebo, Regent of the Thembu. It was a position Jongintaba had secured in part with the backing of Hendry Mandela, a royal counsellor. Jongintaba lived in relative splendour at the seat of the Thembu royal family called Mqhekezweni, The Great Place. It was here that Mandela was introduced to many things that were to have a profound impact on him. It was in Mqhekezweni that Mandela sat around the fire listening to the tribal elders tell stories of great African kings and warriors. He has often reflected on the impact such stories had on his young character: 'Many years ago, when I was a boy brought up in my village in the Transkei, I listened to the elders of the tribe telling stories about the good old days, before the arrival of the white man. Then our people lived peacefully, under the democratic rule of their kings and their *amapakati*, and moved freely and confidently up and down the country without let or hindrance. Then the country was ours, in our own name and right. We occupied the land, the forests, the rivers; we extracted the mineral wealth beneath the soil and all the riches of this beautiful country.'

It was in Mqhekezweni, too, that Mandela – secretly at first – sat in on the tribal council meetings of the Thembu. People travelled many miles to attend such meetings and each person was given an opportunity to speak. Decisions were only reached by consensus or were delayed until a future meeting. It was here, where he shared a hut with Jongintaba's son Justice, that Mandela blossomed as a student and where he underwent circumcision.

the early years

BECAUSE MANDELA'S FATHER had been a royal counsellor, it was planned that Mandela would be trained to fulfil a similar function for the young Thembu king, Sabata. Consequently, he was sent, together with Justice, to the renowned Methodist institution of Clarkebury and then on to the even more highly regarded Healdtown. It was here, at Healdtown, in about 1938, that Mandela first heard of an organisation called the African National Congress (ANC). Mandela graduated from Healdtown and went on to study court interpreting at the South African Native College of Fort Hare in 1939. Being a court interpreter was considered a highly prestigious post at that time, especially in the rural areas.

Mandela enjoyed cross-country running and was a fine boxer. He joined Fort Hare's ballroom-dancing fraternity and signed up for the drama society. He was not especially interested in politics in those days but was certainly aware of developments in South Africa and in the world at large. Before he could graduate from Fort Hare, however, Mandela became caught up in student activism – although it was still not political activism – and was, in fact, expelled for leading a protest against bad food.

At about this time, the Regent informed Mandela and Justice that he was dying and that before he died he wanted to see the two young men married and settled. Wives had been chosen for both of them, he explained. But neither Justice nor Mandela approved of the choices or of the manner in which their prospective brides had been selected. They were modern young men who wanted to make their own decisions in this regard. To avoid the pending finalisation of their marriages, Justice and Mandela ran away from home and found themselves hundreds of miles away in Johannesburg, the city of gold, looking for work.

After taking up a post as a policeman on the mines, Mandela fortuitously met a young estate agent in Johannesburg by the name of Walter Sisulu. They immediately

▲ Mandela's second marriage, in June 1958, was to the young and vivacious social worker, Winnie Madikizela.

took a liking to each other and Sisulu, who heard of Mandela's wish to be a lawyer, soon arranged for Mandela to begin his articles at the offices of local firm Witkin, Sidelsky & Eidelman. 'Stay out of politics,' were Lazar Sidelsky's famous words of warning when Mandela first started out at the law firm.

comrades in arms

MANDELA WORKED FOR THE FIRM during the day, studied at night and lived in a backroom in noisy and dirty Alexandra. According to Mandela, this was the most difficult period in his life. Hungry, poor, hardworking and dressed in a threadbare hand-me-down suit, he eked out a living in the harsh post-war city, and some days he would walk the 12 miles to work and back to save his bus fare. It was certainly during this time that he became aware of the day-to-day injustices that were an inevitable and indeed deliberate consequence of the system soon to be formally known as apartheid. He described his awakening in his autobiography, *Long Walk to Freedom*: 'A thousand slights, a thousand indignities and a thousand unremembered moments produced in me an anger, a rebelliousness, a desire to fight the system that imprisoned my people.'

It was during this time that he was introduced to a young nurse, Evelyn Mase, a cousin of Sisulu, and Mandela was instantly attracted to her. They were married in 1944 and, after sharing a house for a short while with Evelyn's brother, moved into their own home in Orlando near Johannesburg. The young couple had three children, a son Thembi, a daughter who died in infancy, and Makaziwe, also a daughter.

In spite of the tough conditions at home and war abroad, change was in the air during the 1940s. The Atlantic Charter signed by US President Teddy Roosevelt and British Prime Minister Winston Churchill 'reaffirmed faith in the dignity of each human' along with several other principles of democracy. This was soon adapted at home into the *African Claims* document, which was to become the founding basis of ANC policy and included a Bill of Rights together with a call for universal franchise. The 1940s also witnessed the African Mineworkers Strike, the Alexandra bus boycott, the entrenchment of the 'Hertzog Bills' of the 1930s, the Italian invasion of Ethiopia, the Durban race riots, the Passive Resistance Campaign and the coming to power, in 1948, of DF Malan's National Party.

All these developments formed the backdrop to the creation of the ANC Youth League. During the 1940s, Mandela rubbed shoulders with some deeply influential political leaders and organisers such as Gaur Radebe, Anton Lembede, Walter Sisulu, Oliver Tambo, and members of the Communist Party, Transvaal Indian Congress and Natal Indian Congress. The ANC, which had fallen back into a moderate slumber in the

▲ Together Mandela and Oliver Tambo set up Mandela & Tambo, the country's first black law firm, and from this sprang a lifelong friendship and political commitment.

1920s and 1930s, was catalysed into radical activism by the Programme of Action adopted by the Youth League in 1949. The Programme of Action spawned the Defiance Campaign – and head-on confrontation with the apartheid state.

Mandela was elected to the executive committee of the Youth League, was appointed national volunteer-in-chief and chairman of the Action Committee and Volunteer Board of the Defiance Campaign. The campaign set out deliberately to break apartheid laws and court arrest. By the end of the campaign, 8 500 people of all races had been thrown in jail for defying apartheid laws.

behind prison bars

MANDELA SUFFERED his first period in jail during the Defiance Campaign and was arrested again on 30 July 1952 under the Suppression of Communism Act. He had, however, never joined the Communist Party and, in his earlier days, had in fact rather enjoyed breaking up Communist Party meetings. He was later to say he was attracted by the notion of a classless society, but that this was as much an appreciation for the classlessness and equality of traditional African social organisation as it was an approval of Marxist ideology. He told the Pretoria Supreme Court in 1964: 'I have been influenced by Marxist thought, but this is also true of many of the leaders of the new independent states. Such widely different persons as Gandhi, Nehru, Nkrumah and Nasser all acknowledge this fact. We all accept the need for some form of socialism to enable our people to catch up with the advanced countries of the world and to overcome their legacy of extreme poverty. But this does not mean we are Marxists.'

Mandela was, however, beginning to pay an increasing personal toll for his political involvement. He rather painfully remembers Evelyn being asked by five-year-old Thembi: 'Where does Daddy live?' Neither was the burden to lighten. Deeply saddened by his mother Nosekeni's continuing state of destitution, he 'wondered not for the first time … whether one was ever justified in neglecting the welfare of one's own family in order to fight for the welfare of others'. It was to be the one sacrifice that was to haunt him throughout his life.

As the passage of apartheid laws was intensified in the early 1950s and bills prohibiting mixed marriages, mixed residential areas and mixed voters' rolls were passed, so the intensity of resistance grew. By the time South Africa's famous Congress of the People met in Kliptown in 1955 to draft a charter for a non-racial, democratic future (the Freedom Charter), Mandela had been served banning orders and was not allowed to appear in public. He was to receive three such orders before he was arrested in front of his children at dawn

▼ In 1952 Mandela and other delegates, including Ruth First, the wife of Joe Slovo, gathered in Bloemfontein to choose between a 'convention' and a 'congress'.

▲ As a young man in Johannesburg, Mandela – intrigued by the skill of attack and retreat boxing required – was able to pursue a passion for the sport he had picked up at Fort Hare.

on 5 December 1956 and charged with treason in a massively public trial involving no fewer than 155 other defendants.

On returning home on bail during the treason trial, he found his home empty and Evelyn and the children gone. Mandela had opened a lawyer's practice in Johannesburg with his friend and ANC colleague Oliver Tambo, but the demands of political work on both Mandela and Tambo, including the incarceration and long trial period, undermined the financial viability of their business. They were the first two black lawyers to open their own practice in South Africa.

After separating from Evelyn, who became more interested in religion than politics and who struggled to accept the demands made on her husband's time and life by the ANC, Mandela drove past a young woman at a bus stop and was immediately entranced. Her name was Nomzamo Winnifred Madikizela. 'At that moment I knew I wanted her as my wife,' Mandela wrote in his autobiography. On 14 June 1958, Mandela and Winnie – as she became known – were married. But marital bliss was never to be on the cards for this activist couple. Winnie herself was arrested in a protest against the passbooks black South Africans were forced to carry to identify themselves and set off on her own course of anti-apartheid resistance. The couple had two daughters, Zindzi and Zeni.

Discussions about shifting from passive to violent resistance took place within the ANC throughout the 1950s. It was a deeply divisive notion. As the years passed, and the stayaways, strikes and marches were met by an 'iron hand', so Mandela began to rethink his own attitude to violence. 'Non-violence was not a moral principle but a strategy,' he wrote later.

In the wake of the Sharpeville massacre in 1960 and following the banning of the ANC and other anti-apartheid organisations soon thereafter, Mandela and his colleagues agreed to forge ahead with a military structure, Umkhonto we Sizwe (Spear of the Nation) in order to intensify the struggle. After Mandela's final acquittal on treason charges in 1961, he went underground to work full time at the building of these military structures, of which he was commander in chief. 'I had no choice but to become an outlaw,' he wrote in *Long Walk to Freedom*. Neither was it something he especially relished: it was hazardous and he was kept apart from his family, 'but when a man is denied the right to live the life he believes in, he has no choice.'

the toll of apartheid

FOR NEARLY TWO YEARS, Mandela evaded the apartheid authorities. He went for military training in Ethiopia, visited Europe and several countries on the African continent and crisscrossed South Africa in disguise. He met with sugar workers in Natal, Muslims in the Cape and held secret meetings in townships and homes from one end of the country to the other. He would call newspapers from telephone booths after narrowly evading capture and it wasn't long before the press dubbed him the Black Pimpernel. 'He was to become more famous in the shadows than he had ever been in broad daylight,' wrote Anthony Sampson in *Mandela: The Authorised Biography*.

The solitude and constant fear of arrest, however, took its own heavy toll on Mandela. As he was to tell the court in 1962, 'It has not been easy for me during this past period to separate myself from my wife and children, to say goodbye to the good old days when, at the end of a strenuous day at an office, I could look forward to joining my family at the dinner table, and instead to take up the life of a man hunted continuously by the police, living separated from those who are closest to me, in my own country, facing continually the hazards of detection and of arrest.'

Mandela's dangerous, glamorous life underground as the Black Pimpernel soon came to end after he was betrayed and captured by the authorities in 1962. He was charged with travelling illegally out of the country and incitement to strike, and arrived at court in traditional dress, wearing a leopard-skin kaross, 'literally carrying on my back the history, culture and heritage of my people.' He was sentenced to three years for inciting and two years for leaving the country illegally, without the possibility of parole.

▼ Mandela's mother, Nosekeni Fanny (pictured here with Zindzi), attended parts of the Rivonia trial with Winnie, but she was to see her son only once when he was in prison.

banished to the island

IN JAIL, MANDELA PROTESTED the obligatory wearing of shorts by African prisoners. He was placed in solitary confinement for his troubles – in a cell perpetually lit by one bulb. For weeks he was utterly isolated, with nothing to read, no means of writing and no one to talk to. 'Every hour seemed like a year,' he wrote later. 'I found myself on the verge of initiating conversations with a cockroach.'

After six months in jail in Pretoria, Mandela was shipped off to the dreaded Robben Island. He had heard tales of the Island since he was a child, listening to the elders around the fire at Mqhekezweni. He heard then how Makanna, the commander of the Xhosa army, had drowned while trying to escape the island and how Autshumao, the Khoi leader, had been banished there. Later, the Island had been used as a leper colony and lunatic asylum. In 1962, Robben Island was a tough, brutal place. But after only a few weeks, Mandela was back in Pretoria. The high command of Umkhonto we Sizwe (MK) had been arrested at Liliesleaf Farm in Rivonia and Mandela and his fellow defendants were to be put on trial for their lives. In October 1963, at the outset of the trial known as the Rivonia Trial, lawyers gave Mandela a 50/50 chance of escaping the hangman's noose. Mandela's famous statement from the dock, a four-hour speech delivered on Monday, 20 April 1964, in which he told the court he was willing to die for his principles, echoed around the world. He ended the speech with an extraordinarily powerful declaration of his convictions:

'During my lifetime I have dedicated myself to this struggle of the African people. I have fought against white domination, and I have fought against black domination. I have cherished the ideal of a democratic and free society in which all persons live together in harmony with equal opportunities. It is an ideal which I hope to live for and to achieve. But if needs be, it is an ideal for which I am prepared to die.'

On 12 June 1964, Mandela evaded the noose but was faced with a life sentence. At midnight, he was flown back to Robben Island in an old military aircraft. His monumental prison sentence, which would total some 27 years, had begun in earnest.

The story of Mandela's imprisonment is one of great hardship mixed with great endeavour. It is a story of the indomitable human spirit, of the triumph of utter conviction and of the faith and collective strength of comrades. 'We were face to face with the realisation that our life would be unredeemably grim,' Mandela wrote of his early days on the Island. 'Prison life is about routine: each day like the one before; each week like the one before it, so that the months and the years blend into each other.'

The struggle against apartheid for Mandela and his colleagues shifted realms from the public to the private. Instead of speeches and rallies, the Islanders taught themselves and each other. Instead of defiance against the police and against apartheid laws, they waged a continual struggle

▲ On Robben Island, Mandela and his comrade Walter Sisulu were considered the leaders of the Rivonia trialists and, in fact, all political prisoners incarcerated there.

with the prison authorities for better conditions, better food and more rights. Underpinning their actions was the unwavering belief that morality was on their side and that they would, one day, be free: 'I always knew that one day I would feel once again the grass under my feet and walk in the sunshine as a free man.'

From behind bars, Mandela heard of the travails that beset his family and especially Winnie. Her letters and visits were a lifeline to hope, but they were also a reminder of his incapacity and helplessness. When Mandela heard that his eldest son, Thembi, had been killed in a car accident and was prevented from attending the funeral, 'it left a hole in my heart that can never be filled.' Prison, said Mandela, is a crucible that tests a person's character to its limit. The most terrible walls are the walls that grow up in the mind, he wrote of his trials on the Island.

In April 1982, after almost 20 years in prison, the commanding officer of Robben Island came to Mandela's cell and told him to pack his bags. He was being moved off the Island to Pollsmoor Prison on the mainland. In the real world, things were beginning to change. Unprecedented levels of civil insurrection and resistance were being met with military force. During the 1980s South Africa became a battleground and Mandela increasingly was being considered the one way out of the dilemma.

The ANC had to contend with the collapse of the Soviet Union and the consequent loss of support. Its military operations against the apartheid state had been largely ineffective and the ANC was no nearer to provoking the spontaneous revolutionary insurrection it had initially believed was inevitable. The Nkomati Accord signed with neighbouring countries damaged the ANC's capacity to operate from the frontline states. The organisation had reached its own 'dead end' and it too needed Mandela to lead the way.

freedom for all

THE DISCUSSIONS BETWEEN MANDELA and officials of the apartheid state over how to move forward took place over many years. Progress was slow, but proceeded nonetheless. The government pushed Mandela to accept his freedom, but attached to his release a range of conditions limiting where he could live or what he could do. In a response to one such conditional offer, read out to a packed Jabulani stadium in Soweto on 10 February 1985 by his daughter Zindzi, Mandela said: 'I cherish my own freedom dearly, but I care even more for your freedom … Your freedom and mine cannot be separated. I will return.'

As time went by, Mandela's conditions improved until, in December 1988, he was moved into a prison warder's house. Then, after President PW Botha suffered a stroke in January 1989 and FW de Klerk took the reins of apartheid power, the tide turned.

On 2 February 1990, President De Klerk met the conditions necessary for negotiations to begin in earnest about the future of South Africa. He unbanned the ANC together with the other liberation movements, released political prisoners and suspended capital punishment. And then, finally, on 11 February 1990, Mandela – at the age of 71 and after more than 10 000 days in jail – walked free.

He steadfastly refused to acknowledge he had done anything other than urge the apartheid government to meet with the ANC. In his first speech as a free man, he told the thousands of people who had gathered to greet him in Cape Town: 'Today I wish to report to you that my talks with the government have been aimed at normalising the political situation in the country. We have not as yet begun discussing the basic demands of the struggle. I wish to stress that I myself have at no time entered into negotiations about the future of our country except to insist on a meeting between the ANC and the government.'

For more than four years, the negotiations between the ANC, the apartheid government and the other party leaders and organisations in South Africa continued. At times, they were close to collapse; at others, it seemed the country was on the very brink of agreement. Political violence and uncertainty plagued ordinary people and convinced the world that a racial civil war was imminent.

▼ In 1977, the apartheid government allowed a media contingent to visit Robben Island and the occasion allowed a rare opportunity to photograph what prison authorities referred to as just another 'prisoner in the garden'.

Then, on 27 April 1994, millions of South Africans voted in the first non-racial, democratic election in the country's history. Mandela was elected president with overwhelming support from the nation and from his party. In his victory speech in Johannesburg's Carlton Hotel, he told supporters: 'This is one of the most important moments in the life of our country. I stand here before you filled with deep pride and joy – pride in the ordinary, humble people of this country. You have shown such a calm, patient determination to reclaim this country as your own. What joy that we can proudly proclaim from the rooftops – free at last!'

leading the people

▲ In the run-up to the first democratic election, Mandela was joined by ANC stalwart Alan Boesak on a campaign tour of Cape Town, Boesak's home territory.

MANDELA'S INAUGURATION was one of South Africa's proudest and most memorable days. No one who was there will ever forget the excited build-up from before dawn or the arrival at Pretoria's Union Buildings of one limousine after another carrying heads of state from around the world. None will forget the tens of thousands of people crammed into the tiered garden of the Union Buildings, the tall figure of Mandela with his two deputies, FW de Klerk and Thabo Mbeki. And especially none will forget the fly-by of South African airforce jets trailing the national colours from their wings in acknowledgement of their new commander-in-chief, nor the roar of a low-flying jumbo filling the ears of the crowd with thunder and the hearts of a nation with pride.

'The time for the healing of the wounds has come,' Mandela told his people and the millions around the globe who watched the day unfold. 'The moment to bridge the chasms that divide us has come. The time to build is upon us. We have, at last, achieved our political emancipation … Never, never and never again shall it be that this beautiful land will again experience the oppression of one by another and suffer the indignity of being the skunk of the world. Let freedom reign! The sun shall never set on so glorious a human achievement! God Bless Africa!'

It didn't take long for Mandela to appreciate the enormity of the task ahead. When he arrived at his new presidential office at the Union Buildings for his first day of work, all the furniture and even the telephones had been removed. This was really a case of starting from scratch, not just in healing a divided and wounded nation, but in administering a complex, modern state with little experience of how things worked. Fortunately, Mandela was surrounded by a cadre of highly capable and now publicly mandated leaders and the task of rebuilding was begun with gusto.

◄ Mandela's presidency saw a renewed sense of spirit in both the man and his people. Here he breaks into his trademark Madiba jive with the dancers of *Woza Africa*.

The five years in which Mandela held South Africa's supreme post were far from easy. Criminal violence, the developmental backlog of three centuries of racial oppression and the demands of governing a modern state at the turn of the 20th century proved to be very real tests. Certainly, progress was made on many fronts, not least in rehabilitating a distorted, struggling economy and in beginning to address the most basic needs of a long-deprived people. Three years after he took the helm as president, he was able to announce: 'We take immense pride and joy in the fact that since 27 April 1994, millions have for the first time experienced access to clean water, electricity, housing subsidies, free health care, nutrition programmes and land.'

As hard as the material improvement of many people's lives had proved to be, there were other hallmarks of success, such as political peace, a new democratic constitution and the basis for racial reconciliation. As he told Parliament in 1999, 'Our transition has been managed with such success that some generously invoke the imagery of "miracle". Things such as equality, the right to vote in free and fair elections and freedom of speech, many of us now take for granted. Many past difficulties are now mere footnotes of history.' Indeed, Mandela's success in achieving the 'miracle' of South Africa's transition from apartheid to democracy won him and former president FW de Klerk the Nobel Peace Prize in 1993.

truth and reconciliation

IN A BID TO RESOLVE the pain and trauma of a divided and often violent past, Mandela appointed a Truth and Reconciliation Commission (TRC) in 1996, chaired by the indefatigable Archbishop Desmond Tutu, himself a Nobel Peace Prize laureate. The aims of the TRC were threefold: to give the victims of serious abuses a chance to tell their stories and find out about the circumstances of their ill-treatment, to give perpetrators an opportunity to unburden their own guilt by sharing the truth and full extent of their actions, and to provide reparations for the victims and their families.

The process, which received vast coverage in local and international media, was controversial and far from flawless, but by the time the final report had been completed, there was no question that it had achieved what it had set out to do: it had given 20 000 people the chance to share their grief and anger and, in so doing, had laid the platform for a peaceful, reconciled nation with a new sense of self-worth and of patriotism. 'We are one people with one destiny,' Mandela told fellow South Africans on Freedom Day, 1998.

Mandela divorced Winnie, from whom he had moved irreconcilably, and later fell in love and married once more. This time, he chose Graça Machel, the widow of Mozambique's late president, Samora Machel, and a cabinet minister in her own right. Few who saw them together doubted the deep love, empathy and respect that underpinned their union.

After a single term, Mandela stepped down as president of South Africa. It was an act many leaders of liberation movements in Africa have found almost impossible to carry through. But it was a passing gift that once again defined Mandela as a man of

▲ In 1993, Mandela and former president FW de Klerk – the two conciliatory figures in South Africa's recent political history – were awarded the Nobel Peace Prize in Oslo, Norway.

destiny and of conscience, and one who refused to compromise his principles. Certainly, he could look back on his term of office as South Africa's first black, democratically elected president with great pride.

'We have laid the foundation for a better life,' he told Parliament at its final sitting of the Mandela presidential term in March 1999. 'Things that were unimaginable a few years ago have become everyday reality. Of this we must be proud ... To the extent that I have been able to achieve anything, I know that this is because I am the product of the people of South Africa. I am the product of the rural masses who inspired in me the pride in our past and the spirit of resistance. I am the product of the workers of South Africa who, in the mines, factories, fields and offices of our country, have pursued the principle that the interests of each are founded in the common interest of all. I am the product of South Africa's intelligentsia, of every colour, who have laboured to give our society knowledge of itself and to fashion our people's aspirations into a realisable dream. I am the product of South Africa's businesspeople – in industry and agriculture, commerce and finance – whose spirit of enterprise has helped turn our country's immense natural resources into the wealth of our nation.'

In the years after his retirement from formal politics, Mandela shifted his gaze to new challenges, new fronts. In the first few months of his presidency, he had established a children's fund with the aim of undertaking work to improve the lives of the little people with whom he so obviously had such a close bond. There was no easier way to bring a broad smile to Mandela's face than when he was surrounded by laughing, babbling children. He was never happier than when he sat at home back in Qunu with his grandchildren playing at his knee. As a public symbol of his determination to improve the lot of South Africa's children, he pledged to pay R150 000 of his salary into the Nelson Mandela Children's Fund every year. This he did, soon building the Fund's endowment and adding to it with his legendary fundraising skills to considerable proportions. The Fund has since played a powerful role in commissioning research and undertaking projects that have benefited thousands and thousands of children, not just in South Africa but across the world. 'There can be no keener revelation of a society's soul than the way in which it treats its children,' Mandela once said.

father of the nation

ANOTHER VITAL FOCUS for Mandela in his post-political years was the matter of the scourge of HIV/Aids. Though a matter of concern during his presidency, it was to be a matter of dedicated action for Mandela in his retirement years, at times sparking tensions with a government that exhibited an occasionally ambivalent attitude to the phenomenon. 'The time has come for South Africans to make a concerted effort to fight the stigmatisation of those who are HIV-positive, those who are dying of Aids. And it is time for South Africans to stop saying that it is someone else's responsibility to combat this illness,' he told the Congress of South African Trade Unions' executive committee in July 2001.

▲ A beaming Mandela greets a jubilant crowd from the balcony of Cape Town's City Hall.

As his health began to deteriorate, Mandela nonetheless ensured that work continued apace to commemorate and celebrate South African history and the achievements of its people and their leaders. The Nelson Mandela Foundation, with its international branches, high-profile trustees and its Centre for Memory, is dedicated precisely to this task. None appreciate the value of a true history as keenly as Mandela himself: 'When the history of our struggle is written, it will tell a glorious tale of African solidarity, of Africans' adherence to principles. It will tell a moving story of the sacrifices of the peoples of our continent made to ensure that that intolerable insult to human dignity, the apartheid crime against humanity, became a thing of the past.'

When Mandela was a small boy listening to stories by the fire, he dreamed one day of being an African hero like Makanna or Autshumao, whose feats of strength and endeavour would save his people. So things have turned out. He has done this not with the power to wield a spear or the strength to kill a foe, but with weapons far more powerful and far more enduring. He has put his enemies to flight and saved his nation with love, forgiveness and understanding.

On the death of his father, Gadla Hendry Mphakanyiswa, the nine-year-old Nelson Rolihlahla Mandela was taken from his family home in Qunu and placed in the care of Jongintaba Dalindyebo, the paramount chief of the Thembu people, who had offered to be the young Mandela's guardian. Jongintaba was based at Mqhekezweni – The Great Place – and it was here, in what the youngster considered the biggest and most impressive hut he had ever seen, that the boy spent what, by all accounts, was a happy childhood. His youth was a traditional one, a time spent playing with the other boys and learning the skills required of a boy in rural Transkei.

What made Rolihlahla's childhood somewhat different to that of most of the boys of Qunu and other villages in Transkei was that his parents, the Christian Nosekeni Fanny and traditionalist Gadla Hendry, as well as his guardian Jongintaba believed firmly in the value of a sound education. So it was that the young Nelson was sent to school and then to college, first in Healdtown and then, at the age of 21, on to Fort Hare.

Fort Hare had no more than 150 students, who were considered the finest black scholars in the country. It was while Mandela was at Fort Hare that he encountered a number of individuals who would not only leave a deep impression on the young man, but also many who would rise to play pivotal roles in black society and the struggle for freedom, among them the likes of Oliver Tambo, DDT Jabavu and ZK Matthews. It was here, too, that he befriended Kaiser Matanzima and the two struck up a close bond. Coincidentally, Matanzima was Mandela's nephew – and as the elder of the two, Mandela's senior – and he too was to play his part in South African history when he became prime minister of the 'homeland' of Transkei created by the National Party's apartheid government in its implementation of its policy of 'separate development'.

After settling in Johannesburg and taking a job as an articled clerk in a prominent law firm, Mandela finally enrolled at the University of the Witwatersrand in 1943. It was a path that would stand him in good stead in the years that followed and it was here, too, that he would meet and develop relationships with anti-apartheid activists such as Bram Fischer, George Bizos and Joe Slovo.

Once the young Nelson Mandela had settled in Johannesburg, he needed to find a steady job, but these were scarce in the big city, especially for a black man. Fortunately, however, it was at this time that he met a young estate agent who was quickly making a name for himself as an astute businessman and respected leader in the community. That man was Walter Sisulu, and the two would quickly become not only firm friends but brothers and comrades in the struggle. In fact, it was at Sisulu's home that Mandela met Walter's young cousin, Evelyn Mase, whom he would marry in 1944, the same year Walter married Albertina. Both Nelson and Evelyn formed part of the Sisulus' wedding party: Mandela stands far left and Evelyn flanking the groom.

The early 1950s saw Mandela and his comrades clash with apartheid authorities when they launched the Campaign for Defiance Against Unjust Laws, a programme of action that would see 'non-white' South Africans purposefully transgress racist laws laid down by the government in the implementation of apartheid. During this Defiance Campaign, Mandela, along with some 8 500 others, was arrested and endured his first brief period behind bars. Here Walter Sisulu (left), Mandela (centre) and Harrison Motlana (right) prepare to appear in court during the much-publicised hearings relating to the Defiance Campaign. The campaign signalled a new era in the struggle, one that showed ordinary South Africans the power of a united front and one that saw many new members enrol in what was slowly emerging as a leading light in the fight for freedom: the African National Congress (ANC).

Mandela's courtship and subsequent marriage to the young nurse Evelyn Mase represented a happy and contented time for the young man. Evelyn was a gentle, reserved woman with an endearing smile and deep religious conviction. In Mandela's own words, she was also a devoted wife and mother and – despite the fact that she was not at all motivated by politics – proved to be a welcome support for her increasingly political husband. Within a year of their marriage, she gave birth to their son Thembi and, a year later, a daughter, Makaziwe. Sadly, the infant died at nine months and, despite a second daughter – also named Makaziwe (Maki) – in 1953 and then a second son, Makgatho, so did the Mandelas' marriage. Mandela's political obligations simply proved too much for the retiring Evelyn and the couple were finally divorced.

Mandela's son Thembi and daughter Maki had grown accustomed to their father's absences from home and the apparent deterioration of their parents' marriage. Nevertheless, they were clearly devastated when, after the first time he was arrested for treason, Mandela returned home to find that Evelyn had made her final break, choosing her faith over her husband's political aspirations. Although Mandela was devoted to his children, he is said – despite his disappointments in the growing lad – to have had a special bond with his eldest one. It was with intense sadness then that, in 1969, when Mandela had been on Robben Island for just five years, he received news that his beloved Thembi had been killed in a car accident. Mandela was devastated, and inconsolable.

Increasingly active on the political front and equally busy as partner in the law firm Mandela & Tambo with friend, colleague and comrade Oliver Tambo, Mandela had quickly emerged as a leader in the resistance against the prohibitive apartheid laws. His increasing visibility, though, meant that he soon became a target of the apartheid government and he was eventually banned, forbidden to appear in public in any sort of leadership role. Finally, in December 1956, he was arrested, charged with treason and, along with 155 others, endured a protracted legal process that would be recorded in the history books as the Treason Trial. The trial proved both long and arduous and it is during this time that Mandela resurrected his passion for boxing, retreating virtually every evening to the gym run by featherweight champion Jerry Moloi, who acted as his sparring partner.

In 1957, during the trying times of the Treason Trial, Mandela met Winnie Madikizela, a shy but glamorous social worker 16 years his junior. Although Mandela's marriage to Evelyn had not yet officially been dissolved, it was already over in all but paper, and it was clear that he was smitten with the pretty 22-year-old, and she with him. Although Winnie's family did not see how this union could last and her father warned her that Mandela was married, first and foremost, to the struggle, on 14 June 1958, just a year after they met, Nelson Rolihlahla Mandela married Nomzamo Winnifred Madikizela. Their marriage – by all accounts, a happy one – was to endure for some 35 years, for 27 of which the two were separated, with Mandela in prison and Winnie – eventually equally as active as her revolutionary husband – either banished or banned or, for all intents and purposes, abandoned. During Mandela's imprisonment, however, it is no surprise that the passion began to wane and although they cherished the same ideals and hopes for a democratic South Africa, they had grown accustomed to living separate lives and different lifestyles, and, following a series of disagreements, they were finally divorced in 1996.

On 21 March 1960, the horror of the massacre by the police of 69 people protesting against the pass laws in Sharpeville brought home not only to Mandela and the ANC but also the rest of the country – black and white – the seriousness of the situation in South Africa. Sharpeville and its aftermath would prove to be a turning point in the country's history and is commemorated today as Human Rights Day. Immediately afterwards, Mandela along with comrades Walter Sisulu, Joe Slovo and Duma Nokwe consulted with ANC president Chief Albert Luthuli, and they decided on a public demonstration condemning the tragedy at Sharpeville and protesting the continuing pass system. Prominent leaders, including Luthuli, Sisulu and Mandela, brazenly burnt their passbooks – a challenge the government did not hesitate to take up. A State of Emergency was declared and a number of arrests were promptly made. One of the first on their list was Nelson Mandela, and within a week both the ANC and the PAC were banned under the notorious Suppression of Communism Act. Throughout this tumultuous period the lengthy Treason Trial continued unabated, even as Mandela was held in custody in Pretoria under the new Emergency regulations – a situation that would last until the end of August 1960, when the State of Emergency was lifted and the accused were permitted to return home.

Following the extended Treason Trial, it was clear that Mandela and his comrades were seen as a serious threat by the National Party government. It was with little surprise, then, that the apartheid forces kept a watchful eye on their whereabouts and activities. With the ANC receiving more and more recognition abroad and the government closely monitoring the comings and goings of the organisation's members, Mandela and a handful of his comrades went underground and established Umkhonto we Sizwe (Spear of the Nation). They were constantly on the move, hiding out at safe houses dotted across the city. Very often, they were compelled to adopt some sort of disguise, and Mandela in turn decided not to shave. In the media attention that followed his going underground, the elusive Mandela was known as the Black Pimpernel. At the end of the year, after attending a conference in Addis Ababa with a delegation of ANC leaders, Mandela stopped off in London with Oliver Tambo, where they were shown around the city by staunch anti-apartheid activist Mary Benson.

The Addis Ababa conference in 1962 provided an ideal opportunity for the ANC to tell the world, and especially Africa, about its activities and aims, and solicit support for its ideals. Afterwards, Mandela embarked on a further campaign to spread the word about the organisation and its aims, and visited a number of African countries, including Egypt, Morocco, Mali, Guinea, Sierra Leone and Liberia. After his stopover in London, Mandela returned to Ethiopia, where he received military training, but after just eight weeks, he was summoned back to South Africa by the ANC – a dangerous move that would prove disastrous. Just days after returning to Liliesleaf Farm in Rivonia, where he had been hiding out as a gardener, Mandela set off to Durban to meet with Luthuli and other leaders of the ANC. It was on his return trip, acting as chauffeur to stage director Cecil Williams, that the South African government finally caught up with him and Nelson Mandela was arrested.

During the trial that followed his arrest Mandela conducted his own defence and, in defiance of what was essentially a white court ruled by a white judiciary, appeared at the opening arguments on 22 October 1962 dressed in the traditional regalia of a Xhosa prince. The court, not unexpectedly, disregarded his forceful statement and he was sentenced to five years in prison for leaving the country illegally and inciting workers to strike.

▲ Just months into his sentence, Mandela heard that Liliesleaf Farm had been raided and that members of the High Command, including Walter Sisulu, Govan Mbeki and Ahmed Kathrada, had been arrested. They had gathered in Rivonia to finalise the further implementation of the armed struggle – a programme dubbed Operation Mayibuye – and had been detained under the Sabotage Bill. Mandela himself was implicated by documents in his handwriting left behind on Liliesleaf, and so the stage was set for what became known as the Rivonia Trial. Sabotage carried a heavy sentence and it seemed inevitable that the accused would face the death penalty. When judgement was passed nearly a year after the arrests it was with some relief that Mandela and his comrades heard that they would serve life imprisonment. In court that day was Mandela's long-suffering mother Nosekeni Fanny, accompanied by Winnie and the children. It would be a long, long time before either could spend any real time with him again. The conviction and sentence would prove to be yet another turning point, not only in the lives of Mandela and his comrades but also in the history of the country.

▶ The men convicted at the Rivonia Trial started serving their sentences in Pretoria, but after only a few days they were placed in handcuffs and leg-irons and transported to Robben Island. Here they were prisoners in every sense of the word: isolated from their families and the rest of society, allowed few liberties or luxuries, and forced to wear standard prison shorts. This was clearly not going to be easy, but one comfort was that, for the most part, Mandela and his comrades were at least able to face the prospect of a lifetime in prison together. Life on Robben Island was tough, with the prisoners compelled to work long hours in hard conditions and while conditions for some of them did indeed improve over the years, those incarcerated on Robben Island would spend their days doing manual labour. For Mandela, for a significant number of years, it meant working, breaking stones and busying himself in the Island's lime quarries.

Images of Mandela during his prison years are few, partly simply because he was incarcerated and separated from family, friends and the media, and partly because he remained a 'banned' person, and the media were thus forbidden to publish either photographs of him or words attributed to him. Apart from the images released after the orchestrated press visit in 1977, few others are known to exist: one is of Mandela and Sisulu in the prison courtyard (see page 12), another of Mandela sewing (see page 35) and yet another of two rows of prisoners in the same courtyard (above). Mandela is said to be fifth from the left in the top row.

Throughout Mandela's incarceration, his comrades and anti-apartheid activists across the globe continued to campaign for his freedom and that of other political prisoners detained by the National Party government. Year after year, their efforts continued without bearing much fruit, but it has been widely acknowledged that the dogged determination of these stalwarts eventually added to the international pressure exerted by world powers on the apartheid government.

While contact was limited throughout Mandela's years on Robben Island, he and Winnie corresponded with painstaking regularity. Mostly, they discussed the children and family matters, but when it came to the struggle and the activities of their comrades they developed a code that eluded the authorities' eagle eyes. When Winnie was herself incarcerated – at The Fort – she was able to send her husband a Christmas wish, along with portraits of the two of them bearing their respective prison numbers. Winnie remained Mandela's link to his family and the world, and their devotion to each other, it seems, never waned. Mandela kept a striking photograph of Winnie on his bookshelf to remind him of her and her dedication – both to him and the struggle.

▲ The imprisonment of the Rivonia trialists sent shock waves around the world but, over the years of their imprisonment, it was Nelson Mandela who would emerge as the figurehead, the icon of the struggle for freedom and democracy in South Africa. Having started his sentence at the age of 46, every year that passed meant that it became less and less likely that he would – or could – maintain a leadership role should he ever be released. In fact, considering the National Party's fierce determination to curb his influence, there were very real fears that he might die in prison, which would make him a martyr among his followers. Throughout his 27-year incarceration, however, there were repeated calls for his release and there were times when many political observers felt that that could indeed be possible. But the apartheid government remained steadfast, and patently ignored the regular protests and marches across the globe calling for Mandela's unconditional release. London, in fact, became a prominent base for anti-apartheid activists, who regularly demonstrated outside the South African Embassy in the city.

▶ After endless media and popular speculation about Mandela's imminent release, President FW de Klerk announced at the Opening of Parliament on 2 February 1990 that all political organisations would be legalised and that political prisoners were to be released, including – much to everyone's amazement, despite the predictions – Nelson Mandela. And just over a week later, on 11 February 1990, Mandela walked out of Victor Verster prison hand in hand with his wife Winnie and faced a frenzied media. Free at last!

Mandela's release after 27 years behind bars finally signalled the turnaround South Africa and the international community had long hoped for. His freedom – and that of others released at around the same time – meant that the country was able to start on that long walk to reconciliation. Swarmed by an adoring following and swamped by representatives of what must have been hundreds of media organisations, Mandela and his party made their way to Cape Town's City Hall on the Grand Parade where he addressed the crowds that had gathered in celebration. This was the first time he had made a public appearance in nearly 30 years, and he was to make the most of his jubilant homecoming. Flanked by his good friends and ANC stalwarts Walter Sisulu and Cyril Ramaphosa, he began, 'Friends, comrades and fellow South Africans, I greet you in the name of peace, democracy and freedom for all ...' and went on to emphasise the importance of the negotiation process that would inevitably follow: 'We express the hope that a climate conducive to a negotiated settlement would be created soon ...'.

The negotiation process, which by necessity had to include representatives of as many South Africans as possible, proved to be as tough and as eventful as could have been predicted. Having to consider the views of so many individuals meant that there was much to discuss, amend and compromise and there were more than a few predictions that the country would face a bloodbath before the talks could proceed. South Africans would, however, by and large, prove the opposite and despite run-ins with both De Klerk of the National Party and Mangosuthu Buthelezi of the Inkatha Freedom Party, negotiations moved forward.

◀ Having attended a special Welcome Home rally in Soweto soon after his release, there was little doubt that Mandela had endeared himself to his constituency and it was clear where their loyalties lay. At that homecoming, he had been astonished at the many thousands who had come to greet him. Standing alongside him was Winnie flanked by Ahmed Kathrada, and Walter Sisulu on his left, and together they raised their fists in victory. There was little speculation as to the outcome of the extensive election campaign that was to take place in the run-up to democracy.

▲ ▶ Before that momentous day, however, two critical events cut to the very heart of Nelson Mandela and his comrades in the ANC, both of which could have halted – or at least hindered – the sensitive negotiation process. The first was the brutal slaying of Chris Hani (toted by many political observers as a strong runner-up as Mandela's successor) by rightwing extremists intent on derailing the negotiation process, and the second the sudden passing of longtime president of the ANC, Oliver Tambo, whom Mandela had personally welcomed back from exile in December 1990 (above). Fortunately, the two leading figures – Mandela and De Klerk (overleaf) and their respective advisors – agreed that neither tragedy would jeopardise the talks that were already underway.

General elections and the formation of a new government – one that would become known as the Government of National Unity – would mean an entirely new era in the history of South Africa, but first there was an election campaign to be run and Mandela had to refamiliarise himself with both the country and its people. So, as the campaign began in earnest, he made his way around the country, giving the world that was waiting with bated breath some idea of the iconic status he would be afforded in the years that were to follow. Nelson Mandela, in a South Africa that was about to change so dramatically as to be almost unrecognisable in its social and political structure, became hero, father, confidante and favourite uncle to millions of South Africans and millions more abroad.

◄ Just weeks before the country went to the polls, Mandela and a small group of fellow prisoners returned to Robben Island to commemorate their stay there and revisit the cells that had been their home for decades. He and other of the accused in the Rivonia Trial – from left, Dennis Goldberg, Andrew Mlangeni, Mandela, Ahmed Kathrada and Walter Sisulu – made their way through the maze of corridors, and across the courtyards and barren quarry in which they had laboured for hours on end.

▼ Mandela, in turn, demonstrated what the prisoners were required to do to the limestone in the Island's quarries, and explained how the fine dust and perpetual glare had contributed much to the deterioration of his eyesight in the years that were to follow.

▲ Freedom Day – as it would be commemorated in the democratic South Africa – dawned on 27 April 1994, when South Africans of all races finally made their way to the polls to cast their votes. For many South Africans – including Mandela himself – this would be their first election, the first time they had been permitted to cast a vote and the first time they would see a black president preside over a truly democratic republic. Following days of joy and jubilation, debate and discussion, the not-unexpected results were announced: Nelson Mandela's ANC had won a resounding victory and South Africa had finally emerged into a new era of freedom.

▶ Mandela's inauguration was set for 10 May, and Archbishop Desmond Tutu – long a defender of human rights and avid campaigner against apartheid – wasted little time in presenting the new president to the citizens of Cape Town, the two stalwarts of the struggle holding hands and raising them in victory.

Nelson Rolihlahla Mandela was sworn in as the country's first democratically elected president on 10 May 1994, 30 years after he was imprisoned on Robben Island by the apartheid government for conspiring against the people of South Africa. Flanked by his deputies, Thabo Mbeki and FW de Klerk, Mandela took the Oath of Office before a massive audience at the Union Buildings in Pretoria, watched by what is said to have been more than a billion people on television worldwide. In attendance were thousands of foreign dignitaries and government representatives, princes and presidents, kings and queens, clergy and sportspeople, singers and artists.

In December 1994, Mandela presented his long-awaited autobiography *Long Walk to Freedom*, the book that would bring his remarkable story to the world. Its launch, attended by many of his fellow prisoners, including close friend and comrade Walter Sisulu, shed some light on the many years of his incarceration and the ideas and ideals that drove him during this time. Naturally, the book became an instant bestseller, acclaimed by historians as one of the most important pieces of literature to emerge from Africa in recent times.

◄ Just a year into the new democracy, new hope and renewed patriotism seemed to be at fever pitch. Never before had there been such optimism for the future of South Africa and its people. As if to emphasise and celebrate this newfound enthusiasm, South Africa hosted the world's top rugby teams in the 1995 Rugby World Cup. The event itself was cause for much celebration both locally and abroad, even more so when it seemed certain that the Springboks would at least get to play in the semifinals. But the South African players went even further. In a nail-biting finish that had even the most disinterested South Africans at the edge of their seats, the Springboks pulled it off and – to an explosion of cheers from ecstatic fans – marched off the field with a 15–12 victory over arch-rivals, New Zealand's All Blacks. In what has been described as one of the most heart-warming moments in recent sporting history, a beaming President Nelson Mandela, wearing a No. 6 rugby jersey (a replica of that of the Springbok captain, Francois Pienaar), presented the coveted Webb Ellis trophy to the equally thrilled Pienaar and his teammates.

◀ ▲ With his ever-increasing popularity both at home and abroad, Mandela's tenure as president saw him tackle an extensive – and, undoubtedly, exhausting – series of state visits. Very soon after his inauguration, he embarked on a number of major tours, the purpose of which were twofold – to cement existing ties with nations with which South Africa already had a friendly and beneficial history and to establish new relationships that would carry the country into the new millennium. Mandela's itinerary often took him a long way from both his official residence at Westbrook and his modest, newly built red-brick home (modelled on the house at Victor Verster prison where he spent his last years as prisoner) in Qunu. In July 1996, he embarked on an official visit to the United Kingdom, where he was hosted by Her Majesty Queen Elizabeth. To celebrate the occasion, Mandela and Her Majesty proceeded down The Mall after visiting the Horse Guard, after which he was accompanied by the Duke of Edinburgh as he inspected the Guard of Honour formed by the Irish Guards.

◄ The years following the inauguration of the president of the newly democratic republic meant not only laying the foundations for the new democracy and establishing sound relationships with the rest of the world, but also putting to rest the ghosts of the past and reconnecting with all South Africans, irrespective of their personal viewpoints or political motivation. In August 1995, Mandela made one of the most remarkable gestures of goodwill the country had yet seen when he took further steps toward reconciliation by visiting the self-styled 'white homeland' of Orania. Here he not only met with Carl Boshoff, leader of the small white community, but – to the astonishment of the world – visited the statue of Hendrik Verwoerd, considered by many to be the architect of apartheid, and took tea with Verwoerd's aged widow, Betsie Verwoerd. The move was hailed the world over as one of the most magnanimous steps ever taken by a world leader in forgiveness of the atrocities visited upon his people, and even Mandela's critics acknowledged the significance of such a step in the healing of South Africa's wounds.

▲ The smiling Betsie Verwoerd, however, belied the many difficulties encountered by Mandela on his journey toward reconciliation. Predictably, one of the greatest obstacles was any sort of conciliatory gesture from former state president PW Botha. When Botha pointedly refused to testify at the Truth and Reconciliation Commission, Mandela made a special trip to George to discuss the issue with the former statesman face to face. Botha, however, refused to budge, and the issue was never resolved.

For Nelson Mandela, travelling the globe meant audiences with a host of heads of state, royalty, religious leaders, film stars, singers and other celebrities. While these visits generally formed part of Mandela's goodwill tours and afforded him the opportunity to pay his respects, for the many celebrities who clamoured to meet him it was an opportunity to meet the man who was being hailed by the international media as the statesman of the decade.

On 17 March 1997, Mandela welcomed Diana, Princess of Wales, to Genadendal, the president's official residence in Cape Town, and is said to have been deeply saddened by the princess's sudden death just 18 months later. In June, the following year, Mandela had an audience with Pope John Paul II at the Vatican in Rome and then, on 26 October 2004, he met with the Dalai Lama. The meeting was an especially poignant one, considering the personal history of the two men and what they had had to endure to ensure freedom, both literally and figuratively, for their people.

▲ Naturally, international politics played an important part of Mandela's new role. Apart from being called upon to mediate on various political fronts in a troubled Africa, he was also expected to rub shoulders with the leaders of the Western world, most notably the United States and United Kingdom, both of which were outspoken critics of apartheid, providing important bases from which the anti-apartheid lobbies operated, but most notably, too, at the forefront of the social and economic sanctions faced by the National Party government in the dim days of segregation.

◀ In March 1998, Bill Clinton accompanied Mandela on his return to Robben Island, where the American president could experience first hand what Mandela had felt and seen and done all those years on the Island. By this time, Mandela was nearing the end of his term in office and Clinton was into his last. This, however, would not be their last meeting. In 2003, both Clinton and British prime minister Tony Blair were at Mandela's side when he addressed an audience at Westminster in celebration of the centenary of the Rhodes Trust and the establishment of the Mandela Rhodes Foundation.

▶ High on Mandela's list of priorities is the issue of HIV/Aids and the scourge that it has become worldwide, especially in Africa. Having seen the scars that the virus has left on his own country and experienced the pain of losing friends and family to Aids-related illnesses, Mandela has chosen to champion the cause both locally and internationally. On 29 November 2003, he joined U2's Bono and a host of international luminaries in what became known as the Mandela 46664 Benefit Concert, a massive and widely publicised series of performances in Cape Town by some of the world's top recording artists to highlight the issue of HIV/Aids and the plight of those living with the illness

On his visit to Palestine in October 1999, Mandela was given a hero's welcome, and he publicly acknowledged that his trip was a 'realisation of a dream ... to come and pledge my solidarity with my friend Yasser Arafat', emphasising that 'the histories of our two peoples correspond in such painful and poignant ways that I intensely feel myself at home amongst my compatriots'.

Much the same may also be said of Mandela's relationship with Castro. His affiliation with Cuba's longstanding leader and his people stems from active Cuban intervention during the darkest days of the struggle. 'Cuban internationalists,' Mandela is said to have stated, 'have done so much for African independence, freedom and justice.' As a result, there is a fondness and sincerity in this friendship that is hard to ignore.

Fortunately, most of Mandela's informal relationships are, for the most part, far less controversial in nature. One such friendship is with American talk-show host, Oprah Winfrey. Mandela calls her 'a queen' and she refers to him as her hero. Winfrey is passionate about the country, its people and its future, so it came as little surprise that it was Mandela who was invited to turn the sod at the launch of the US$10-million Oprah Winfrey Leadership Academy for Girls at Henley-on-Klip, Gauteng, in December 2002. The academy welcomed its first intake of girls in 2007.

As an avid boxer in his youth, Mandela seemed equally delighted to meet world champion Mohammed Ali at a dinner in Mandela's honour at the Tribeca Grill in New York in May 2005. The two, neither quite as sturdy on their feet as they had been at their athletic best, sparred playfully for the cameras, egged on by a host of Hollywood stars and celebrities also in attendance.

After so many years in confinement, suffering through long absences from home and missing out on the normality of an ordinary life, Mandela places family high on his list of priorities. Even well into his retirement he continued to travel extensively and relinquished much of his personal time to carry out the duties either imposed on him as Father of the Nation or accepted willingly as peacemaker and defender of human rights. In his twilight years, however, things have changed considerably. Mandela appears to spend more and more time with family and close friends. He seems to take great delight in those rare moments that allow him to enjoy what it is like to be a husband, father and grandfather and to forget, just for a while, the issues with which he has to contend as a statesman and politician.

▲ In May 1990, just months after his release, he returned to his ancestral home in Qunu. Here, for the first time in three decades, he was able to reminisce on family life in rural Transkei and spend time with his children and grandchildren, including little Bambatha, born while his grandfather was still a prisoner of the state. Then, just three months after his return to his family home in Qunu, Mandela met Graça Machel, widow of Samora Machel, president of Mozambique from 1975 until his untimely death in a plane crash in 1986. By 1995, there was a surprising new development in the personal life of Mandela when he made public his burgeoning relationship with the gracious Graça Machel, 27 years younger, but in every other way his equal. As the months passed, it became clear that the two were clearly smitten and it was not long before they were seen holding hands and even kissing in front of photographers.

▶ In 1998, Mandela celebrated his 80th birthday and, following weeks of media and public speculation, announced his marriage to his Graça. The dual celebration, at which Mandela's grandson, Mandla, toasted his grandfather and his new wife, took place amid spectacular fanfare at Gallagher Estate outside Johannesburg, where the Mandelas were joined by 2 000 well-wishers. On an equally celebratory note, in April 2007, Mandla (son of Makgatho) reclaimed the family's traditional role as *inkosi* (chief), head of the Mveso Traditional Council and one of six kings of the Xhosa people, a position lost by his great-grandfather, Hendry, in the early 1900s and renounced by his grandfather in favour of national politics and a lifetime of struggling for the freedom of all South Africans.

◀ ▲ The birthday and wedding were also celebrated in style in the Kruger National Park, where the clearly jubilant Mandela improvised with his trademark Madiba jive with local Shangaan dancers in traditional dress. In fact, life with Graça introduced a whole new dimension to Mandela's life. While he continued to play an advisory role in state affairs and remained constantly on the go, he also appeared to be more relaxed and seemed to delight in the company of his new wife.

▶ Nevertheless, duties continued to call and in a symbolic gesture in November 1999, following what must have been one of the most difficult times of the post-election period, Archbishop Emeritus Desmond Tutu, who headed up the Truth and Reconciliation Commission, handed over the Commission's official report to Mandela.

◀ No matter what Mandela's home life may have demanded of him during his term in office and while he continued to play an active role as president, he had already announced his successor at the ANC's triannual conference in December 1997 and by early 1999 it was clear that he was beginning to take a back seat to presidential candidate, Thabo Mbeki, widely hailed by his comrades as the best individual to succeed Mandela as the country's head of state in the elections that were to take place that year. Mbeki had already stepped forward to take the reigns, his candidacy endorsed by Mandela and the ANC executive.

▶ As arduous as the election trail was, Mandela did not slow down. Instead, he threw his full effort behind the ANC and its policies, accompanying the president elect and Jacob Zuma, the man toted to be Mbeki's deputy, on a number of vote-canvassing missions among constituents. Whatever the outcome of those results, it was evident that Thabo Mbeki had large boots to fill and a legacy that would be difficult to follow.

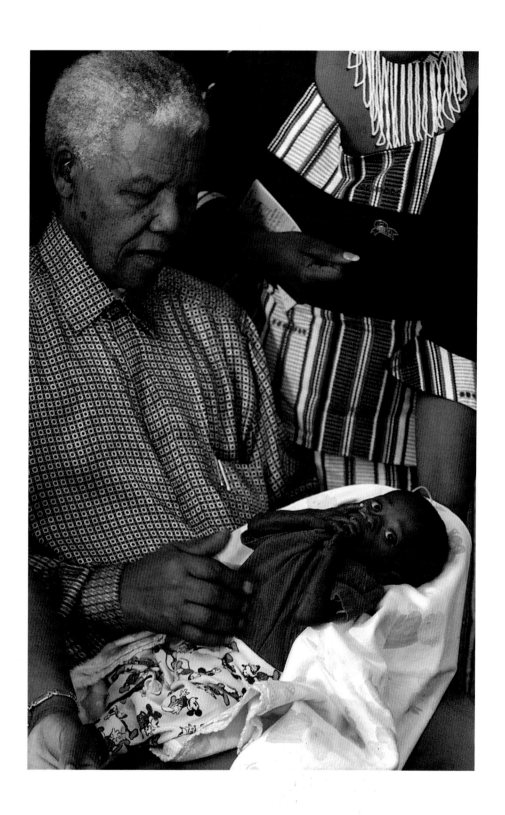

◀ ▲ With Thabo Mbeki officially installed as the country's new president, Mandela – while hardly divorcing himself entirely from affairs of state – was at last able to divert his attention to issues and projects that had been compelled to take a back seat until his official retirement. One such issue continued to be the role of HIV/Aids in Africa, particularly South Africa, where the infection rate has become the cause of alarm to many observers. Mandela has thrown his full support behind this particular cause, and has developed a solidarity with Zackie Achmat, the prominent HIV-positive Aids activist and leader of the Treatment Action Campaign. In December 2001, he visited Beautiful Gate, a centre that cares for children in Crossroads, Cape Town, where he took a six-month-old infant infected with the virus into his arms.

▶ Despite his unofficial duties and countless public engagements, however, there are times when he is able to slip away from the public eye and out of the spotlight to take some time out. He generally celebrates his birthdays in Qunu with close members of his family, but also hosts large groups of schoolchildren for special birthday festivities. In July 2003, Mandela celebrated not only his 85th birthday with family and friends in Johannesburg, but also his and Graça's fifth wedding anniversary. In attendance were songstress Yvonne Chaka Chaka, long a favourite of both Mandela and Graça, and Adelaide Tambo, the widow of his dear friend Oliver, who had been Mandela's predecessor as leader of the ANC during the exile years and a devoted colleague and comrade during Mandela's time in prison.

◄ ▲ Mandela's 85th birthday was celebrated throughout the country. In Johannesburg, he and Graça were presented with a mammoth cake, as well as good number of smaller ones that allowed the Mandelas to share the event with plenty of well-wishers. It is on occasions such as family birthdays that Mandela gets to spend quality time with his extended family. The following year, 2004, saw Mandela and his wife of six years, Graça Machel – to everyone's amazement, 'Mrs Mandela' has retained the surname of her late husband, Samora Machel – attend a celebration in Johannesburg, where the former president was granted the Freedom of the City. Also sharing the day with the couple was Mandela's ex-wife Winnie Madikizela-Mandela. While no one beyond the immediate family will truly understand the relationship between Mandela and Winnie and between Graça and Winnie, by all accounts the festivities were jovial and relaxed, with no hint of tension between them. In fact, they showed a united front and were quite happily photographed together.

▶ Festivities continued in May 2004 when it was announced in Zürich, Switzerland, that South Africa had been approved as host country for the FIFA World Cup in 2010. South Africa's bid committee had pulled out all the stops to ensure that the country would be awarded the rare honour, inviting some of South Africa's brightest luminaries to the announcement event broadcast live across the globe. Among them, of course, were Nelson Mandela and Archbishop Emeritus Desmond Tutu, both ardent soccer fans and champions of the South African cause.

Mandela's legacy has, in many ways, become a pivotal part of South Africa's social, cultural and political heritage and both the Nelson Mandela Foundation and the Nelson Mandela Centre of Memory have tried to assemble and preserve the archival material on which that heritage centres. In 2004, the *466/64: A Prisoner Working in the Garden* exhibition aimed to do just that: preserve the documented record of the ex-prisoner's life. Among the images presented to Mandela on the occasion was a gift from fellow-prisoner Mac Maharaj: a framed portrait of a naked woman running. The photograph had featured in an issue of *National Geographic* all those years ago and Mandela's comrades had given it to him for his birthday 40 years previously. It then took pride of place on the desk of Prisoner 466/64, Nelson Mandela. Another image was that of Mandela and other 'prisoners in the garden', taken when a media contingent visited Robben Island in the 1970s.

▲ The dawning of 2005 saw Mandela face one of the greatest sadnesses of his adult life, certainly of the post-apartheid years. While still in prison, he had faced the death of his eldest son, Thembi, and prison authorities refused to allow him to attend the funeral. In January 2005, Mandela then lost another of his sons, Makgatho, a devastating loss alleviated only by the fact that this time he was free – in every sense of the word – to attend Makgatho's funeral. He and Graça made the trip to Qunu to pay their final respects, and bravely announced that his son had died from an Aids-related illness.

▶ Just six months later, Mandela – by now generally seen walking with the aid of a walking stick – had more to smile about when he celebrated his 87th birthday. As usual, Graça was by his side and the intimate festivities shifted gear to become a grand-scale celebration when he attended the third Nelson Mandela Annual Lecture in Johannesburg. Mandela was presented with a white cake with four candles, which he blew out to loud applause from the audience, while a jubilant Archbishop Tutu led an impromptu rendition of 'Happy Birthday'.

▲ ▶ All this time, Mandela continued to have both a public and private life. Although he was well in retirement, there would be constant calls for public appearances and invitations to large-scale media events. At the same time, however, his audiences with high-profile individuals, such as he had enjoyed at Genadendal with Kofi Annan, Secretary-General of the United Nations, were downscaled in order for him to slow down, and the seemingly endless string of royalty, statesmen and celebrities clamouring to meet with him was severely restricted, most especially by his ever-vigilant assistant, Zelda le Grange. Just as she had tended to him during his busiest years, Le Grange has continued to ensure that Mandela's life runs as smoothly as possible. As he has become less sprightly and more reliant on her, she accompanies him virtually wherever he goes, always at hand to make sure that he is comfortable and in need of nothing.

▶ With Thabo Mbeki firmly at the helm (overleaf), Mandela finally stepped aside to enjoy – at least some of the time – a more private life that would allow him to relax, reminisce and reflect on his life and the contribution he has made, both as an individual and as a representative of the people. Mandela has never been shy to admit that democracy, equality and freedom were achieved not by one person but by the collective. He has always been emphatic that the struggle was never just about Tambo, Mandela or Sisulu and what they sought to achieve.

ACKNOWLEDGEMENTS

The brief quotations and extracts reproduced here come largely from
Nelson Mandela: From Freedom to the Future – Tributes and Speeches edited
by Kader Asmal, David Chidester and Wilmot James (Jonathan Ball, 2003).
Acknowledgement is also made of the following publications:
Adrian Hadland, *Nelson Mandela – The Prisoner Who Gave the World Hope* (Short Books, 2003)
The Nelson Mandela Foundation, *A Prisoner in the Garden* (Penguin, 2006)
Nelson Mandela, *Long Walk to Freedom – The Autobiography of Nelson Mandela* (Macdonald Purnell, 1994)
Anthony Sampson, *Mandela – The Authorised Biography* (HarperCollins, 1999)
Elinor Sisulu, *Walter and Albertina Sisulu – In Our Lifetime* (David Philip, 2002)

PHOTOGRAPHS

Cape Argus / Trace Images: pp. 40, 81; *Drum* / Bailey's African History Archives: pp. 29, 34; Gallo Images / Gettyimages.com: pp. 7, 76–77, 90, 91;
Brenton Geach (*Cape Argus*) / Trace Images: p. 93; Benny Gool / Trace Images: pp. 4–5, 14, 38–39, 49 (bottom), 50–51;
Bob Gosani / Bailey's African History Archives: p. 25; Louise Gubb / Trace Images: front cover, pp. 15, 41, 42–43, 43 (top), 44–45, 46, 47, 48–49, 50 (top),
52 (top and bottom), 53, 67 (top), 68, 69, 72–73, 74, 84, 85; Independent Newspapers / Trace Images: p. 59; INPRA pp. 1, 2–3, 17, 20, 26, 36 (top), 38 (top),
54–55, 56, 57, 60 (top and bottom), 61–62, 62 (top), 66 (top), 67 (bottom), 70–71, 75, 78–79, 82–83, 96; Sasa Kralj / Trace Images: pp. 61, 92;
National Archives: pp, 36 (bottom), 37 (top and bottom); The Nelson Mandela Foundation: p. 13; PictureNET Africa / AP Photo: pp. 16, 66 (bottom),
86–87, 94–95; PictureNET Africa / Henner Frankenfeld: p. 58; Karen Retief (*Cape Argus*) / Trace Images: pp. 64–65;
Robben Island Museum (Mayibuye Archives): pp. 6 (top and bottom), 10, 11, 12, 18 (top and bottom), 19, 23, 24, 27, 28, 30–31, 31, 32, 33, 35;
Jurgen Schadeberg / Bailey's African History Archives: pp. 8, 22; Sisulu Family Collection: p. 21; Matthew Willman / The Nelson Mandela Foundation: pp. 88, 89;
Eli Weinberg / Bailey's African History Archives: p. 9, back cover; Obed Zilwa / Trace Images: p. 80.